# SENSORY STIMULATION GROUP THERAPY
## for the mentally challenged

~~~~~~~~~~~~~~~~~

## Thomas E. Mall
### (M.A.; M.C.P.S.W.)
~~~~~~~~~~~~~~~~~

SENSORY STIMULATION GROUP
THERAPY
for the mentally challenged


Copyright 2018 by Thomas E. Mall


This book may not be reproduced or transmitted in whole
or in part in any form or by any means, electronic or
mechanical, including photocopying, recording, or by any
information storage and retrieval system, without the
written permission of the publisher, except where permitted
by law.

# DEDICATION

This work is dedicated to those clients with whom I worked in the many nursing homes in the State of Georgia and their contributions to the development of the exercises that provided the learning skills that made this sensory stimulation group therapy a success.

# ~ Author's Note ~

When presented with the challenge of providing bi-weekly therapy to approximately 120 clients in 12 nursing homes, I found it quite impossible to provide one-on one quality interactions. With my research into various models of group work, I developed the form of group therapy presented here. One of the challenges present when working with Mental Health Management Services out of Atlanta, GA, was the primary diagnosis of mental illness that brought our services to these clients. Many of the residents who could benefit from sensory stimulation either did not have a diagnosis that would allow them to receive these services, i.e, had a diagnosis of dementia or Alzheimer's Disease that were not covered under the particular program. The only way to provide the service was to assign them with an alternate, secondary diagnosis that fit the program. We did find that an Alzheimer's diagnosed client did respond very well to the sensory stimulation group therapy, but it was not scientifically measured if the client retained much that was acquired in the therapy session. During the first year of the program, there were two other therapists working with the clients and they too used some of the same themes as I; both reported experiencing similar responses and development. I had one or two of my co-therapists use the same theme as I to see if they observed the same responses and reactions that I did.

Special thanks to Dr. Sheila S. Saperstein for review work and Michael G. Putrow for technical support.

# Table of Contents

# ~ 1 ~

## Sensory Stimulation Introduction

The term Sensory Stimulation as used here means a group of activities to enhance awareness of residents served in nursing homes or long term care facilities through a program developed around a theme.  These activities employ all senses including audio, visual, touch, smell, taste and tactile manipulation of objects.

During sessions at long term care facilities in which the author provided individual and group counseling sessions with residents whose primary diagnoses were mental illnesses, it became evident that another approach might better engage these residents.  Most residents in long term care facilities are elderly; however, some may be children or adolescents diagnosed with developmental disabilities.  The variety of illnesses range from mental retardation to paranoid schizophrenia and, it seems, everything in between.  The task faced was how to reach residents of any age, with a variety of diagnoses in group therapy which is meaningful and will engage them in conversational interaction.

Notwithstanding the individual counseling that is required for residents with acting out behaviors, the clinician is involved with a large caseload of clients during a finite number of hours.  Clinicians are often required to see more patients than can be accommodated in a regular working day.  The answer seems to be including as many as possible in group therapy.  Consequently, a combination of individual and group therapy skills is essential.

The materials presented here are one clinician's answer to working with a large caseload of clients residing in nursing homes and other long term care facilities. Residents are of diverse ages with unique needs, often requiring individual interventions.

In the literature one finds sensory stimulation identified as a resource for group interaction.  This presentation of materials is offered as a guide to exactly what can be done in an individual setting with long term care residents.

Each continuing care site has strengths and limitations in which to develop a sensory stimulation activity.  The older facilities may not have a "group room" in which to hold the sessions.  In that case, a solarium or dining room could be used.  The primary needs of a room or space in which to hold the group is the availability of chairs, a table and TV-VCR for use in audio-visual presentations.  The ideal location should be a self-contained room used for therapy sessions.  That "ideal" is not always present.  Any room will do as long as the essentials described exist.

We often find that other residents are in the area of a common room.  This is reality, since, as a clinician, I am coming into the residents' home to perform counseling sessions, not to interfere with their daily routine.  Nevertheless, when several residents are in the area being used for a sensory stimulation group, I find that they involve themselves as passive participants in the activity.  In actual fact, some do become thoroughly engaged in the activities.

Selection of participants for the sensory stimulation group has been based on residents served by the author's caseload of those with a primary diagnosis of mental illness (other than dementia or Alzheimer's disease).  Other participants are added to form a group of working size; ideally from eight to twelve in number.  The facilities clinical staff is consulted to identify other residents who may benefit from a sensory stimulation exposure.  It is often necessary to present an in-service training for all staff to familiarize them with the program.

This writer's experience in developing the program in one facility ran into opposition from a unit nursing staff supervisor who stated that:  "None of these residents will respond to the intervention".  The author agreed that sometimes a patient may not respond in an outward way to the contact, but one cannot tell what is reaching the subconscious.  An individual session was held with two residents in their room.  Both had diagnoses of mental retardation and cerebral palsy, one with schizophrenia added and the other attention deficit disorder.  An in-room session was held with responses from both residents that included verbalizations, laughing, manipulation of objects and body movements.  Several unit staff were observing from the doorway.  The response of the patients to this intervention was enough to convince the nursing supervisor.

The next visit to the facility was the beginning of sensory stimulation group sessions.  An inservice staff training session was held prior to our first client group session.  This training gave the staff ideas how they could help the residents in their program.

Several resident responses over a twelve month period stand out in this writer's memory.  The first unexpected response was generated from Ms Katheryn.  The resident had been extremely active in the long term care facility, was outgoing and verbal until a massive cerebral vascular accident (CVA) rendered her totally incapacitated.  When the clinician first met Ms Katheryn, he saw her in her room. Little response was generated from this initial contact except for eye movement. The resident was paralyzed on the left side, had lost the capacity for speech and often cried out in apparent pain.  For several months in-room visits took place after clinical records were reviewed.  Every two weeks visits to the facility were made and at each visit the therapist recorded the continued increase in the resident's temperature that was in the range between 99-102 F. degrees.  Nursing staff charted every effort to reduce the fever until finally, after three months, it was down to a normal range and Ms Kathryn could join a group.

At one visit the clinician noticed that the resident was up and out of bed for a beauty parlor appointment to have her hair done.  He asked the staff to bring Ms. Katheryn into the sensory stimulation group.  The theme for this session was: "What did you do  before air-conditioning?"  Several items were used in the session including an electric fan, cardboard 'church' fan and an early 19th century folding fan.  Towards the end of the activities the therapist placed the open historic folding 19th Century fan in front of Ms. Kathryn's face and said:  "Ms Kathryn, would you please show the other residents how you would flirt with your young man using the language of fans that we just discussed -- you know, using your eyes with the "come hither look".  At that point Ms Kathryn gave forth a loud belly laugh that was the first outward response since her stroke.

Ms Kathryn attended almost every sensory stimulation session over the next twelve months with increasingly active participation.  She often smiled at the sight of the clinician, began saying words and connecting words which had meaning to the situation.  Many times she would reach out to grasp the therapist's hand and lightly squeeze it.  That coupled with a smile and positive attention continued through the entire year.

It is a response from clients like Ms Kathryn that keep us going in the field of rehabilitation services.  Another example of response to sensory stimulation group work came from a resident in a nearby long term care facility.  Ms Lou had been institutionalized for most of her 58 years with diagnoses of schizophrenia, mental retardation, adjustment disorder, organic brain syndrome and mixed disturbance of conduct and emotions.  She wore a leg brace with an elevated shoe of which she seemed to be self-conscious. Ms Lou exhibited a hostile expression and behaviors toward other residents and most of the staff. Although she was verbally responsive, the few words she spoke to the therapist when initial contact was made were: "Get out!"! For several months the therapist continued to invite her to sensory stimulation groups without success.

It was learned that Ms Lou enjoyed eating candy, although she had been diagnosed as diabetic. She liked cheese crackers and anything sweet. At each contact the resident was given a 'treat' of a package of cheese crackers or two or three pieces of sugar-free candy: "Oh, is this for me?", she said in response. This coupled with a smile indicated that the protective wall was coming down. A major breakthrough came with the theme, "Easter Parade" in which activities were presented around what one does at the Easter Holiday; e.g., wearing hats, having new clothes, and going to church. A video used was "Easter Parade" with Judy Garland and Fred Astaire.

Ms. Lou had continually been invited to participate in the sensory stimulation group that resulted in her refusal each time. At times, she would walk into the solarium where the program was held, but sit at the far end of the room observing. When she was invited to join the group she always refused. During the Easter theme, she sat close to the group activity for the first time and the therapist noticed her intently watching. When the video, which was cued to the song: "Easter Bonnet", began, Ms lou started to smile, walked towards the T.V. and sang along with the video. Her face became animated with a smile as she joined in with the group activities. She knew the words to the song and began to sing. Later, in other presentations, it was found that Ms. Lou had knowledge of many more lyrics to the songs used in my themes.

Ms Lou had missed few sensory stimulation group therapy sessions. During the following eighteen months, she had decreased her incidents of aggressive behaviors and had increased some socialization skills. Again, we do not suggest that the changes are a direct result of only the group experience, but there have been no other outside variables introduced into her rehabilitation program.

One year later, participants were given clues that the place to be visited was the location of the well known hymn, "Rock of Ages". Ms. Lou continued her growth in the group program with her responses in the theme, "Rock of Ages". She began in an upbeat mood, alert, attentive, smiling; one of her better days. The theme had a photograph of the actual "Rock of Ages" that is located in the Cheddar Gorge, England. Residents were to identify the generic name for what they saw ... a rock. Responses came from several group participants who named the object as a rock. The therapist pulled further information from members and quickly they identified the hymn as "Rock of Ages". Participants were given clues as to the place to be visited was the location of that well-known hymn, "Rock of Ages". The photo was of the actual structure that inspired the song, Rock of Ages. During the session, Ms.

Lou was more verbal than usual, making statement that had meaning.  When the song was identified, she began to sing the words to Rock of Ages and knew the first two verses of the song.  It was becoming more evident that this resident has the ability to identify words and music to songs familiar to her.  At these times, she became very animated and interacted with the rest of the group.

The previous information was experienced with the development of this sensory stimulation group therapy program.  It is here that I'll list some of the themes that have been developed over the past ten years of work with mentally challenged individuals living in twelve separate nursing homes in the State of Georgia.  Many of these themes have also been used by other therapists working with similar clients diagnosed with mental illness in other Georgia nursing homes.  They have reported to me several similar instances of resident responses they have encountered.

It is understood that some of the items that I used are personal to me, as are many of the themes.  My suggestion to anyone using this book will be to find something you find interesting and develop it into a specific theme. Music, videos, familiar object and other topics of interest can be a catalyst to develop any number of themes, so use your imagination.  I've used a video camera to film some themes, some videos on the market and just objects found around the house.  I've tried to limit the length of the sessions to a bout 25 or 30 minutes.  The time used depends upon the attention spans of the participants.

Facilities usually have T.V.'s available to show videos.  If music is used, I always have a small cassette player available to play selections of music.

The themes presented will include items or objects to be used.  If a video is used, the presenter will have to cue up the video to the section needed for the presentation.  At the end of each therapy session, I've always prepared a treat for participants to eat.  This is how we get to use the senses of smell and taste.  Because many of my residents were diabetic, I would bake something that was sugar-free or an item that would not cause any physical harm.  Often, anything that is brought into a facility must be authorized by the administration.  However, each facility has its own rules and regulations.

When we have music, it is always a good idea to have residents move in time with the music or other physical activity like passing objects when trying to identify the use of the object.  There are so many activities that can be included in the themes that it is dependent upon the imagination of the therapist who developed the theme.

The following selection of themes are suggestions only.  The therapist or activities director can develop themes relevant to clients at the facility.

# GOALS OF SENSORY STIMULATION ACTIVITIES

- o   Improve awareness
- o   Prompt functional behaviors
- o   Foster alertness
- o   Create social, environmental responses
- o   Present orienting information
- o   Provide pleasurable experiences
- o   Create emotional, communication and expression

# SENSES TO BE STIMULATED
# THROUGH ACTIVITIES SHOULD
# INCLUDE, BUT NOT BE LIMITED TO:

o    **Smell**

o    **Movement**

o    **Touch**

o    **Vision**

o    **Hearing**

o    **Taste**

o    **Manipulation (Kinetic)**

**(Multisensory--present one sense
or activity at a time)**

**SIZE OF GROUP DEPENDS UPON THE NUMBER OF STAFF AVAILABLE.**

- o    **4 to  6 residents (one person)**
- o    **8 to 10 residents (two people)**

# SUGGESTED TOPIC AREAS



o    **Use of a theme or focus on time of year, holiday, item or feeling invoked through imagery, developed from a song, etc.**

o    **A functional response should be elicited.**

o    **Activities in topics should be presented in a sequential way using the senses.**

# SYMBOLS FOR SENSES
### that will be used in each theme:

S    **SMELL**

T    **TASTE**

V    **VISION**

K    **MANIPULATION (Kinetic)**

A    **AUDIO-HEARING**

# SENSORY
# STIMULATION
# THEMES

### EASTER

A    Tape: Music from Jesus Christ Superstar

    or Her Comes Peter Cottontail (song or video)
(Move in time with music)  Ask: 'What is the  meaning of Easter?(Religious Holiday)
Discuss: What did you do when growing up or with your family at Easter?     (Go to
church, Lent, new clothes,  "Easter Egg Hunt?"
From the religious holiday, "What Happened as it  went commercial?"

A/K    Easter Basket (What is this?) What did you usually
find it? Discuss:  (Basket contains:  Decorated
eggs, stuffed toy bunny, 'squeaking' chicken,
colored easter grass, etc.

V,K    Participants identify each item, pass around and
handle. (Ask:"Was your Easter basket hidden? Did
family members come over for Easter dinner?'

A/V    Video:  Easter Parade…"In Your Easter Bonnet"
(Astaire, Garland) Move in time with music.

S/T    Treat:  Sugar-free shape of egg or rabbit.
Victorian sponge cake with sugar-free jam between
layers. (Determine what is between layers;)

1

## JULY 4, HOLIDAY

A      Music:  "Star-spangled Banner".  Ask:  "What is the name of this song?"  Say: "Francis Scott Key wrote this on a ship in Baltimore harbor during the war of 1812.  The words to the poem became the national anthem."  Can you sing the words to our national anthem?  (sing along with the music)

V/K    Ask:  "How do we celebrate our nation's birthday?"  (parades, fireworks, picnics)  Show mock firecracker.  Striped hats, flags.  Pass items around.  Participants:  Throw firecrackers, wave flags.

A      Music:  Replay: Star-Spangled Banner.  Residents sing along with music.

S/T    Sugar-free cookies  (residents:  I.D. flavor, smell)

------------------------------------------------------------

"Oh, say can you see. By the dawn's early light,
What so proudly we hailed
At the twilight's last gleaming?
Whose broad stripes and bright stars,
Thru the perilous flight,
O're the ramparts we watched,
Were so gallantly streaming,
And the rocket's red glare,
The bombs bursting in air,
Gave proof thru the night that our flag was still there.
Oh say, does that Star Spangled Banner yet wave---O're the land of the free
And the home of the brave?"

<h1 style="text-align:center">CHRISTMAS TRADITIONS</h1>

A    Music:  "Oh Christmas Tree" (or similar) Ask:  What is the name of this song?  It tells you in the words?" (Oh, Christmas Tree), What do you remember from your first Christmas?"  Discuss.

V/K    Miniature tree.  Say:  "Here is a small tree that needs trimming, with what would you trim it?"  (Lights, balls, garlands, etc.) Pass tree around to participants.

V/K    Santa Clause soft doll.  Ask:  "What is this I'm holding? (Santa).  We have several traditions at this holiday, depending upon your beliefs.  It can be a spiritual time, a time for children and Santa Clause, a time for every religion.  Try to remember some of the traditions you had as a child."  Discuss.

V    Video:  The Nutcracker, or It's Christmas-time Charlie Brown.  Move in time with the music for The Nutcracker, enjoy watching Charlie Brown.

S/T    Treat:  Christmas Cookies.  I.D. smell/taste.

---

[2] Holiday Cookies   +                 Christmas Tree

## ST. PATRICK'S DAY

A/K   Music:  Irish Rover.  "The Unicorn".  Move in time with the music.  Ask:  "What country has this kind of music, and what people speak with this accent?" (Ireland)

V   Photo: Rainbow.  Say: "Look very closely at this photo and tell me what you see in the sky. (Rainbow)  According to the Iris, what is found at the end of the Rainbow?" (pot of gold)

V/K   Pot of gold coins.  Say: "Look at the pot of gold, put your hands in the pot and feel the gold coins.  Do you really think there is a pot of gold at the end of the rainbow?"

V/K   Toy leprechaun.  "Irish lore says that there is a little person who guards the gold at the end of the end of the rainbow, who is it?" (a Leprechaun).  Pass around the toy to touch, feel.  "Here is a toy Leprechaun.  Ask:  What is the holiday that is celebrated on March 17th?" (St. Patrick's Day)

V/K   Shamrock.  Pass around, say:  "This is a symbol of St. Patrick's Day--a Shamrock, or three-leafed clover.  St. Patrick came to Ireland from England to convert the residents to become Roman Catholic and used the Shamrock to show the Trinity of the Father, Son and Holy Spirit."  Pass around a cardboard Shamrock.

V   Map and Flag of Ireland.  Say:  "Here is a map of Ireland, you can see that it is located just across the Irish Sea from England.  We also have a flag of Ireland...look at the colors:  green, white and orange."

A/V   "Riverdance". Look at some of the dancing done in Ireland.

S//T   Green shamrock shaped cookies. I.D. smell/taste

3

---

# HAPPY BIRTHDAY

A     Tape:  or play piano: "Happy Birthday"
Ask: "What is this song?" "who has a
Birthday this year?" (everyone)

V/K    Party, hats, favors, balloons etc.  Pass out
items to group, try on the hats.  Say:
"What did you do as a child on your
birthday?  Who remembers having a
party?" Discuss the party.  "Did anyone
get spanked the number of years on his/her
birthday?  What games did you play?  Pin
the tail on the donkey?"

A/V    Who are special people during a birthday
party?  Tell me who they are.  Discuss.
Here is a short video of  Pres. Kennedy's
Birthday with a song by Marilyn Monroe.

K/A    Tape:  Happy Birthday -- sing-a-long.

S/TA Treat:  Birthday cake or cupcakes.

5

---

## RAINBOWS

A      Tape:  "Thunderstorm" (Sound of Nature Tapes).  Ask:  "What is this sound?" (thunder, rain). "what do you see in the sky sometimes after a rain, especially when the sun comes out?"  (Rainbow)

V      Photo:  RAINBOW  Ask:  What colors to you see in a rainbow? Chart of Primary Colors:  "Here are the three primary colors from which all other colors are made:  Red, Yellow, Blue'  I.D. colors.  Can someone tell me what the Bible says is the reason for the rainbow?"  (God's sign, after the Great Floods that the earth would not be destroyed by water (after Noah & the Ark story)  Ask:  "Has anyone every heard that story" Discuss.

V/K      Pot of Gold, Leprechaun--Say:"Irish folk lore tells us something about the rainbow. What do they say is at the end of the rainbow?" (pot of gold).  Show pot of gold pieces or coins.  Participants pick up pieces of gold coins or objects and put back in pot. Ask:  "Who is said to guard the pot of gold at the end of the rainbow ?"  (Leprechaun) Leprechaun doll -- pass around doll to group.

A/V      Video:  "Wizard of Oz".  Judy Garland singing "Over The Rainbow"  Participants sing along with video or music.

S/T      Cake or cupcake with rainbow frosting. I.D.

## BEER--BAVARIA

A/K    Music:  "Beer Barrel Polka" (Frankie
Yankovic or other)  Move in time with the
music, sing along.  (Demonstrate Polka dance)
Ask:  "Anyone know how to do the polka?"
In what country do they dance the polka?"
(Germany, Austria, Belgium).  Ask:  What do
you know about Germany?"

V    Map of Germany.  Show northern and
southern parts of Germany.  Say:  "The
capital of Germany before the WWII was
Bonn, now with the unification of Germany,
it is Berlin>"

V/K    Look at the map to see where Munich is
S    located….this is the heart of Germany--
Bavaria in Southern Germany.  Ask: "For
what product is Germany known?"  (Beer)
Show empty bottle of LOWENBRAU beer.
Pass around and have each member smell
the empty bottle…to I.D. smell.

V/K    Show beer stein.  Open top to show how
stein is used. (or show photo)

V    Pictures of Germany.  Munich, Black Forest
(where cuckoo clocks are made).  Photo of
castles along the Rhine River, King Ludwig's
Castle (from which Disney's Snow-White's
Castle was copied)

ST    Treat:  Apple Strudel….I.D. taste of  apple

7

---

<sup>7</sup> Stein of Beer                    German Flag on display

## BLARNEY CASTLE (KISS THE STONE)

A      Music:  Irish Rovers - "Lily The Pink",
"Whiskey on a Sunday".  Move to the music,
listen to the words, accent of what country?
(Ireland).  Ask: "What holiday is March 17?
(St. Patrick's Day - patron saint of Ireland)

V      Map of Ireland. "Look at the location of
Ireland.  Irish Sea separates Ireland from
England, Scotland and Wales (British Isles)
European Continent is across the British
Channel.

V/K    Toy Leprechaun--Ask:  "What is the name of
this toy?"  (Leprechaun) A toy of the
imaginary little people in folklore.

V/K    Irish Flag.  Ask: "what colors are in this
flag?" (green, white, orange)

V/K    Shamrock.  "This is the symbol of three leaf
clover that St. Patrick used in his teaching
of the Trinity.

V/K    Green Skimmer, green carnation flower.
"Try on hat, carnation in lapel or pinned on
dress." During the St. Patrick Day Parade,
some people will be wearing things like this.

V/K    Video:  "The Enchanting British Isles".
Blarney Castle --Kissing Blarney Stone
to get good luck and gift of gab.

S/T    Treat:  Cookie and green frosting.  ID S/T

---

[8] Kissing Blarney Stone

# PARIS, CITY OF LIGHTS

A     Music:  Edith Piaf "La Vie En Rose"
Ask:  "What language is this and what country? (French, France)  We'll visit Paris, known as 'the city of lights'. Edith Piaf was a street singer who became very famous."

V     Photo of La Tour Eiffel.  Say:  "The Eiffel Tower is on the left Bank in Paris along the Seine River--a symbol of Paris."

V     Photo of Notre Dame Cathedral.  Ask: "Does anyone know the name of this famous Paris cathedral?"  (Notre Dame)

V/K   Map of Paris.  "Notre Dame Cathedral is located on an island between the right bank and the left bank in the Seine River.  Look at the map to find location of the cathedral and the right and left banks of Paris."

V/K   Beret.  Say:  "This little hat is a beret".  Pass this around and try it on.  This is typically a French hat and can be worn by men and women."

S/T   Treat:  Small French bread, spread.  Ask: "What is this and how does it taste"

## A  VISIT TO THE UNITED KINGDOM

A/K    Music:  "God Save Our Queen", national anthem.  Move in time with the music.  Ask: "What song is this?  We know it as: 'My Country 'Tis of Thee'.  It is actually the national anthem of the United Kingdom, we just stole it when we gained our independence from England in 1776.

V    Pictures of England.  Photo of Henry VIII and Queen Elizabeth, I,  Ask:  "Who are these people?"  (Name them for audience) "Henry VIII (1491-1547); He had many wives and took over the church and made it the Anglican Church.  Elizabeth I (1533-1601) was known at the Virgin Queen."

V    Photos of Elizabethan building.  Say: "This picture is of an Elizabethan style building. It is made out of wood and plaster.  This is also known as Tudor and many buildings like this are still in use today."

V    Picture of William Shakespeare.  Ask: "Of who is this a picture?" (Wm Shakespeare) Ever hear of him? The greatest playwright in history."

A/V    Video:  "My Fair Lady".  Play musical and say: "This is a famous musical about a poor girl in London who was a flower girl who wants to become a Lady. Do you recognize the music?"

S/T    Treat. Tea cake.  I.D. smell & taste.

---

9

[10]

_______________________________

[10] Map of Ireland, England - upper left      Big Ben Clock - London

## ROCK OF AGES

V      Photo:  Rock of Ages, Cheddar Gorge.
Ask:  "What is this photo?  Clue: a church
hymn that we all know is titled after this
image.  ROCK.  (Rock of Ages)"

A/K   Tape:  Rock of Ages or play on piano.  Say:
Sing along with the music. Discuss words.
Song was written by Rev. Augustus
Montague Toplady with music by Dr. Thomas
Hastings.  Show copy of music.

V      Map of England show Cheddar Gorge
located in area between Bath & Wells.
Ask:  "What other things come to mind that
may come from the area of CHEDDAR
Gorge?  Yes, Cheddar cheese.  Has anyone
ever eaten cheddar cheese?"

S/T   Treat:  Cheese crackers.  I.D. taste & smell.

"Rock of Ages, cleft for me, let me hide myself in
thee Let the water and the blood from Thy wound- ed side which flowed, be of sin,
the double cure, save from wrath and make me pure.
Could my tears for ever flow. Could my zeal no longer know. These for sin could not
a-tone, Thou must save, and Thou a-tone. In my hand, no price I bring, simply to
Thy cross  I cling.
While I draw this fleeting breath, when my eye lids close in death. When I rise to
worlds unknown, and be-hold Thee on Thy throne. Rock of A-ges, cleft for me, Let
me hide myself in Thee, Let me hide my-self in Thee."

---

[11] Cheddar Gorge Rock of Ages        Cheddar cheese rounds

## 1950's ROCK-N-ROLL

A     Music: "Mr. Sandman".  Ask:  "Do you recall when this song first became popular?  What year?"  (1950's)  "What do you remember from the 1950's?"  (This is when girls were wearing poodle-skirts, hair in  pony-tails or poodle hair cuts.)  Discuss.

V     Photos of boys/girls.  "Time of Elvis Presley & start of Rock-n-Roll.  Boys wear Levi jeans and white socks, D-A haircuts.  Who knows what 'D-A' means? (Duck's Ass).  Discuss:

V/K     Pass around pair white socks.  "Example"

A     Music:  "Love Me Tender"  Ask:  "Who is this singing?" (Elvis Presley).  "Where were school dances held?"  (Gym)  "Called sock-hops because couldn't wear shoes in the gym.  T.V. had 'American Bandstand' hosted by Dick Clark"  Volunteer to show dance steps.  Discuss.

A/V     Video:  "Grease".  Play parts of video.  "Time of hot rods, B&W - T.V.  Ask:  "Do you remember some of the activity at high school?"  Discuss.

S/T     Treats:  Sucker.  I.D. smell, taste

12

**CIVIL WAR (war of northern aggression)**

V     Picture of Margaret Mitchell.  Ask: "Does anyone know what this woman wrote? (clue:  activity about which she wrote took place in 1864.)  She was the author of GONE WITH THE WIND--era of the Civil War."

A     Music:  "Battle Hymn of the Republic" tape or play on piano.  "If you know the words to this song from the Civil War, sing along."
"Mine eyes have seen the glo-ry of the com-ing of the Lord.  He is tramp-ling out the vin-tage where the grapes of wrath are stored, He hath loosed the fate-ful light-ning of His ter-ri-ble swift sword. His truth is march-ing on.  Glo-ry, glo-ry Hal-le-lu-jah! Glo-ry, glo-ry, Hal-le- lu-jah! glo-ry,glo-ry, Hal-le-lu-jah!  His truth is march-ing on."

V     Video:  "Gone With The Wind".  Watch opening of movie to see the life-style and mansion "Terra" Say:  "Look at how the people were dressed and the architecture."  Discuss:

S/T  Treat:  Gingerbread.  I.D. smell and taste.

13

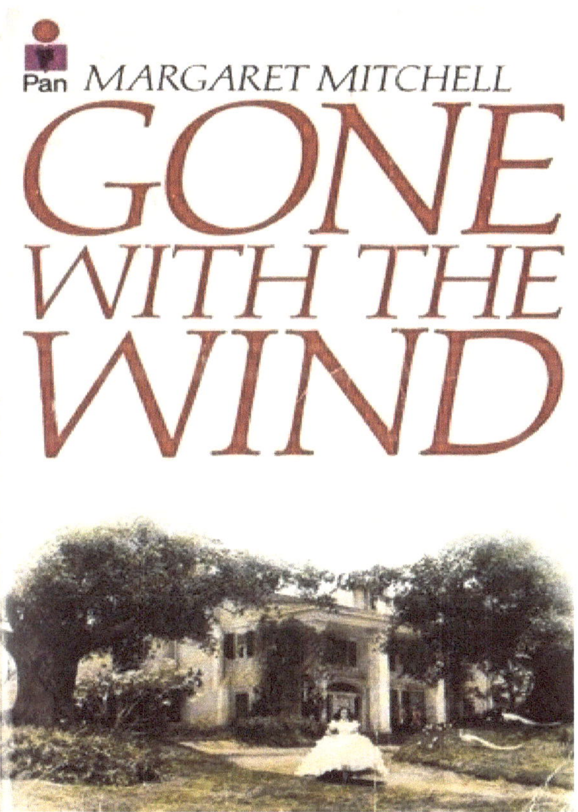



______________________________

[13] Pictured Civil War meeting on the battlefield;     Cover of novel Gone With The Wind- Terra

## CATS

A/K   Music:  "What's New Pussycat?"-Tom Jones.
Ask:  "What's the name of this song by Tom
Jones?"  (What's New Pussycat?") Move in
time with the music. "CATS is the name of
the theme for this session.  Does anyone own a cat?
What kind?"  Discuss:

V   Photo of cats.  Ask:  "What colors are these
cats?  How many different varieties of cats
can you name?"  Discuss.

K/V   "If you were a cat, what would you do?  How
would you move?  Demonstrate movement.
How would you make up your face to look like
a cat?  Has anyone ever seen the film or
stage production of CATS?"

V   Video:  "Cats".  "We'll see how the actors
use make-up and costumes to look like a cat.
The actors have to learn to move like a cat,
use latex rubber on their faces and body to
look like a cat, use stage makeup to change
color of their bodies for the effect."

S/T   Treat:  Cookies that are in the shape of a
mouse...I.D. smell and taste.
"

---

[14] Domestic Cat                 'CATS' from cover of musical

## MAKING HAY

A/K    Music:  Calliope music.  Say:  "Listen
to music, where do you find sounds like
this?  (Fair, carnival)  "Move in time with
the music."

V/K    Hay/Straw.  "Touch material."  Ask: "What
is this, where do you find it? (Hay/Straw)
"Who has lived on a farm, or visited a farm?
What do we mean when we say, 'make hay
while the sun shines?"  Discuss.

V/K    Straw Hat.  "From what are these hats
made?  (Straw) Pass hat around to people.
Try hat on."

V/K    Toy truck/wagon with hay in it.  "Pass wagon
around, feel the straw."  Discuss.

V/K    Scarecrow doll. Pass doll around.  Say:
"What is a 'scarecrow' , How it is used?
(To scare crows/birds)

V/K    Video:  Wizard of Oz.  Play video. Section
with characters dancing down the yellow
brick road.  Discuss characters.

S/T    Treat.  Cheese straws or cheese bits.. I.D.  taste, smell.

**FIREPLACE**

A      Sounds of Nature tape: "Old Fashioned Christmas" Ask: What sounds do you hear? (wood chopping, fire crackling) Our theme for today is Fireplace, wood burning."

V/K    Small twigs or tiny log. Pass materials around to I.D. Ask: "What are these coming and what are they used for? Kindling to start a fire. How many of you had a fire-plact at home? Ask: If you had a fireplace, is there a special time when you had a fire?"

V/K    Bellows. Pass around and ask: "Who knows what this is? What is it used for? (Bellows) It is a bellows that is used to push air to help start a fire.

V/K    Wadded up paper. Ask: "What is this used for when you build a fire?" (to lite with match to begin the fire)

K      Demonstrate laying a fire with paper & twigs but don't light materials in a miniature fire-place. Has anyone been in the Boy or Girl Scouts? Did you learn to build a fire?"

S/T    Treat: Prune whip made with cool whip. I.D. ingredients.

## FARM MARKET - STANDS

A/V    Tape: "Old McDonald Had A Farm".  Sing-
K      a-long.  Participants sing along with music.
       Miniature farm animals, pass around.  Say:
       "Identify the animals that are in the song,
       what sounds to each of these farm animals
       make?  Discuss.

V/K    Ask:  "Has anyone ever lived on a farm?  Tell
       us what it was like."  Discuss.  Ask:  "What
       vegetables are grown on a farm?  What
       animals do we see on a farm here in WI?
       (Photos of vegetables that are grown.)
       Ask:  "What is your favorite vegetable that
       you like to eat?"  Discuss.

K/S    (Veg. and one zucchini from a market stand)
       Pass around and say:  "Smell these Veg.
       "Smell these vegetables and tell us how
       you would prepare them to eat.  Would any
       of these be eaten without cooking?"
       Discuss

V      "Oklahoma" Play opening of video.  Say:
       "Here is the opening of this musical.  Move
       in time with the music."

S/T    Treat:  Zucchini Muffins.  I.D. smell, taste.
       Say:  These are made from zucchini.

---

15

[16]

---

[16] Vegetables on racks in roadside stand        Farm Stand at road side

## FISHING

| | |
|---|---|
| A | Music: "Old Man River" Ask: "Of what does this song remind you? (River) What do you do when you are out in a boat on a river or lake? (fish, swim) When was the last time you went fishing? Is there anyone who has never gone fishing?' Discuss. |
| V/K | Bamboo pole, bait (plastic worm). Ask: What do you need when you go fishing? Discuss: Show pole, bait, hat, etc. Pass items around. Discuss. |
| K | Plastic worm. (bait). "What do you need to put on the hook for fishing? What can we use for bait?" (crickets, grasshoppers, worms, shrimp, lures, etc) |
| V/K | Ask for volunteer to bait hook, throw line into water. (possible another person behind a wall over which baited line is thrown….and tie on plastic fish with other smaller fish inside) |
| V/K | Volunteer pulls line in after a 'bite'. Staff helps volunteer and takes off fish, showing smaller fish inside bigger fish. |
| V/K | Video: "Dorf Goes Fishing" View video section Dorf teaches wife to fish. |
| S/T | Treat: Goldfish crackers…I.D. smell, taste. |

________________

[17] Fishing from pier        Fishing Boats

## BEACH PARTY

A/K Tape: "Vacation" - Connie Francis.  Move in time with the music.  Ask: "What did you do as a youngster in the summer, when not in school?  (various answers)  How many of you went to the beach?  Do you remember some of those Beach Movies with Frankie Avalon, Annette Funicello, Sandra Dee, James Darrin?"

A/V "We are going to the beach, what will we need to take with us?"  Various answers.  "We'll need:  Blanket, pail, shovel, sun screen, bathing suit, radio, hat, etc.  Does anyone remember the song:  "It was an itsey bitsey teenie weenie, yellow polka dot bekini?" Play tape of music.  "Move in time with the music."

K Sand in bucket.  Pass bucket around and have members feel the sand.  Ask:  "How does the sand feel?  Shells in sand.  "Pick out the sea -shells in the sand feel?"

K/V (Beach ball).  "Here is a beach ball, throw ball to one another."

K (Conch shell).."Here is a conch shell.  Pass it around and listen to the 'sea' sound in it."

V BIKINI BEACH video: section on beach.

S/T Treat:  Saltwater taffy.  I.D. smell,taste.

---

18

_______________________________

[18] Sandy Beach                    Beach bonfire at dusk

# HOT AIR BALLOONS

A/K   MUSIC: "Up, up and away" (5th Dimension)
      Ask: "About what is the group singing?
      (Balloons) Move in time with the music."

V/K   Photo of Balloon. "Look at this photo, what
      is it? (Balloon)  What is at the bottom of
      Balloon, it is a place for people to ride.
      What is the name of this thing?" (Gondola).
      Ask: "What makes the balloon go up in the
      air?" (Helium that is lighter than air)

V/K   "Look at the picture of the balloon and tell
      me what colors do you see?" (reds, yellows,
      blue, orange, purple).  In the U.S. the city
      of Albuquerque makes it the balloon capital
      of the world.  Do you think there are people
      inside the gondola?" (yes, they control the
      flight and some are sightseers.)

V     Video: "Around the World in 80 Days"
      Play section of film that shows the balloon
      lifting in the air.

V/K   Have. balloons for client's to blow up.  Ask:
      "Can I have a volunteer to blow up a balloon?
      Give balloon to blow up and help if needed.
      We'll tie a string on balloon so you can take
      it with you." (one or more people and
      balloons)

S/T   Treat:  Round or balloon shaped cookies.
      I.D. shape, smell and taste of cookie.

56

# CHARLESTON - 1920's ERA

A/K   Music:  "Won't you Charleston With Me?"
(from musical The Boyfriend)  Say:  "Move
in time with the music.  (ask) Of what time
in history does this music remind you?"
(1920's)  (demonstrate the Charleston
dance)

V   Flapper dress, feather hat, handbag, photo
of clothes, feather boa  (magazine of the
1920's)  Pass around feather boa.
"Are any of these fashions found today?
Some of the eveningwear can look like these
fashions."

V/K   Magazine showing men's fashions of the
1920's.  Say:  "Sometimes men wore skimmer
straw hats".  Show in costume book or
fashion book.  If have a skimmer, pass around to
try on.

A/V   Video:  "Mame".  Show party with dancing
the Charleston.  Move in time with the music
or move feet like in the dance.

S/T   Treat:  Icebox cookies.  I.D. smell & taste.

### KEEPING COOL (BEFORE A/C)

A/K    Music: "It's Too Darn Hot" - Ella Fitzgerald.
Say: "Fan yourself with your hand.  Before
A/C, how did you keep cool?"  Discuss.

V/K    Small electric fan.  Say: "Here we have a little
electric fan that we may have used to keep cool.
(pass fan around to participants)  I'll plug in the
fan to an electric outlet, but what did we do when
we didn't have electricity?"  (Fan with our hand
or magazine, newspaper)  Discuss.  show fanning
with hand, paper etc.

V/K    Hand held fan, church fan, etc.  Say: "I'll
pass around these fans that were used in early
times and you can fan yourself with them."

V/K    Say: "There was a 'language' of fans the way
women held them in a way to let other know how
they felt,e.g., a woman held fan in front of face
with only eyes showing in a flirtatious way.  Or
she could point closed fan to indicate for someone
to leave or sit."  Demonstrate action.

A    Sound of Nature Tape> Summer.  "Listen to the
sounds on the tape and I.D.

S/T    Treat:  typical summer treat.  I.D. smell/taste

## THE LONE RANGER

A/K    Music: "William Tell Overture"  Ask:  Of what does this music remind you? (Lone Ranger)  Participants to move like riding a horse.  Ask:  This is the William Tell Overture, but when the Lone Ranger film makers used it as background for the film, most people identify it as Lone Ranger."

V/K    Hats, silver bullet, Tonto's head, bank miniature horse, mask.  Look at objects pass around to participants.  Ask: "What was the name of the Lone Ranger's horse? (Silver).  What is the name of Tonto's horse? (Paint)  What is the significance of the silver bullet? (Lone Ranger had a silver mine) Bullet was a symbol of him."

A/V    Video: "The Lone Ranger, Outlaw's Trail
           A broken Match" (or similar)
Discuss.

S/T    Treat:  Trail Mix or peanut butter crackers.  I.D. smell/taste.

### VIDALIA ONIONS

A     Music: "Cry Me A River" (Barbara Streisand)  Ask: "Who knows the name of this song? (Cry Me A River) What vegetable do you think of when you hear this song?  Clue:  When you peel it, tears come to your eyes. " (Onion)

A/V  Map of Georgia.  Say:  "Sometimes if
K/S  the weather is too wet or too cold the farmers get worried that the crop will not be very good.  These are Vidalia Onions." Pass around a Vidalia Onion to smell. On Map, show where onions are grown. "They are grown around Tattnall County, find that county on the map."

A/V  Photo of Vidalia Onions growing in Glennville, Tattnall Co.  Say: "Look at the rows of onions growing.  There is a  patent on the work Vidalia and only those grown in this area can be called Vidalia.  Others can only be termed 'sweet' onions.

S/K  Pass around a slice of Vidalia Onion, Discuss

S/T  Treat:  Small onion roll.  I.D. smell, taste.

VIDALIA
ONIONS

## APRIL SHOWERS

A/K   Music:  "April Showers" on tape or piano. Ask:  "What is the name of this song? What month is this?"  Move in time with the music.

A/K   Rubber boots, rain hat, umbrella.  Pass items around to identify.  Say:  "Try on these items, open the umbrella, and identify the items and how they are used."  Discuss.

A/K   Say:  "Do you remember as a child you might have said this little ditty: 'Rain, rain, go away, come back another day'"?  Ask: "Repeat the ditty."

A/V   "Thunderstorm" - Sound of Nature Tapes. Ask:  What is this noise on the tape? (thunder, rain)

V   Video:  "Singing In The Rain" (That's Entertainment, or film of same name) "Gene Kelly gave another way of looking at the rain".  Move in time with the music.

S/T   Treat:  Popcorn.  I.D. smell and taste.

APRIL
April Showers bring May Flowers
Brenda B. Cremonie

Happy Spring

### BASEBALL (summer games)

V/K   Baseball, glove, cap.  Ask: "Of what does these items make you think?"  (summer games, picnic, watermelon, hot dogs, hamburgers, etc)

A   Music:  "Take Me Out To The Ballgame" Say:  "Move with the music and tell me what is said in the lyrics...'peanuts and crackerjacks..'  Sing along with the music.

K   Soft ball.  "Throw the softball to one another (carefully).  Ask:  "How many of you have ever played baseball as a child?" Discuss.

V   That's Entertainment  (Sinatra & Kelly dancing and singing "Take Me Out To The Ballgame"  (as above)  Sing along with the video.

S/T   Treat:  Crackjacks or popcorn.  I.D. smell and taste.

Helmet, Baseball bat, ball          Baseball Stadium

## BLAISE HAMLET (BRISTOL)

(Blaise Hamlet was a period  16th C. hamlet designed by John Nash adjacent to Blaise Castle. This was an example of a garden suburb, occupied by retired staff of Blaise Castle, built about 1811.)

A/K   Music:  "This Old House" - Rosemary Clooney.  Move in time with the music. Ask:  "Listen to the words, can anyone tell us the name of this song?"  (This Old House)

V/K   Photo of thatched roof cottage (16th C) Say: "Look at the roof of this cottage, it is made of straw or thatching. Thatching is a process of placing straw, rushes, palm leaves to cover a roof.  It is usually about 3 ft. thick.  Think of a nursery story of 'The Three Little Pigs' with one of them making a house out of straw, one twigs, one brick.

V/K   Say:  "Thatched roof cottages built in the 16th C. were made of stone with thatched roofs.  Some roofs were made of slate or other materials.  There was little wood used at that time in England because not much available.

A/V   Pictures are of Blaise Hamlet, near  Bristol. Map of England.  Show where Bristol is located and Blaise Hamlet is east edge of city.

S/T   Treat:  Sugar cookies.  I.D. Smell/taste.

Slate roof cottage                    National Trust Designation

PARTICIPANT EVALUATION

Below is a list of characteristics of each response noted on the documentation record.

o None- No response at all-slept, stared into space without recognition, disengaged
o Poor-Responded at very low level-moved eyes once, turned to face another, attempt
    to interpret sensory message without evidence of success. Participated at low
    Level.
o Moderate- Responded at a moderate level-Maintained eye contact, turned to face
    another, attempted to interpret sensory message and provided feedback to the
    provider and/or member of the group demonstrated some enjoyment.
o High-Responded well- Maintained good eye contact and/or en face position if blind,
    demonstrated ability to manipulate, identify, and interpret data regarding sensory
    Information, clearly enjoyed the session.
o Very High- Responded very well- Remained engaged during the entire session.  Was
    Able to identify and process sensory data without difficulty. 1

| Name | Facility | | Date of Plan |
|---|---|---|---|
| | | | |

| DATE | RESPONSE(Circle one) | PROVIDER | TITLE |
|---|---|---|---|
| / / | NONE  POOR  MODERATE  HIGH  VERY HIGH | | |
| / / | NONE  POOR  MODERATE  HIGH  VERY HIGH | | |
| / / | NONE  POOR  MODERATE  HIGH  VERY HIGH | | |
| / / | NONE  POOR  MODERATE  HIGH  VERY HIGH | | |
| / / | NONE  POOR  MODERATE  HIGH  VERY HIGH | | |
| / / | NONE  POOR  MODERATE  HIGH  VERY HIGH | | |
| / / | NONE  POOR  MODERATE  HIGH  VERY HIGH | | |
| / / | NONE  POOR  MODERATE  HIGH  VERY HIGH | | |
| / / | NONE  POOR  MODERATE  HIGH  VERY HIGH | | |
| / / | NONE  POOR  MODERATE  HIGH  VERY HIGH | | |
| / / | NONE  POOR  MODERATE  HIGH  VERY HIGH | | |
| / / | NONE  POOR  MODERATE  HIGH  VERY HIGH | | |
| / / | NONE  POOR  MODERATE  HIGH  VERY HIGH | | |
| / / | NONE  POOR  MODERATE  HIGH  VERY HIGH | | |
| / / | NONE  POOR  MODERATE  HIGH  VERY HIGH | | |
| / / | NONE  POOR  MODERATE  HIGH  VERY HIGH | | |
| / / | NONE  POOR  MODERATE  HIGH  VERY HIGH | | |
| / / | NONE  POOR  MODERATE  HIGH  VERY HIGH | | |
| / / | NONE  POOR  MODERATE  HIGH  VERY HIGH | | |
| / / | NONE  POOR  MODERATE  HIGH  VERY HIGH | | |
| / / | NONE  POOR  MODERATE  HIGH  VERY HIGH | | |
| / / | NONE  POOR  MODERATE  HIGH  VERY HIGH | | |
| / / | NONE  POOR  MODERATE  HIGH  VERY HIGH | | |
| / / | NONE  POOR  MODERATE  HIGH  VERY HIGH | | |
| / / | NONE  POOR  MODERATE  HIGH  VERY HIGH | | |
| / / | NONE  POOR  MODERATE  HIGH  VERY HIGH | | |

1
MHM Services, Inc. Atlanta, GA Evaluation Form. 2002

Other technique is:  "Time Slips".  Sensory Stimulation as presented here is primarily using sense stimulation and is more specific.

SELECT BIBLIOGRAPHY

Free Images / istock by Gerry / Images / istockphotos.com

MHM Services, Inc.  Atlanta, GA 2000